Between the Lines

illustrated by
Peter Deligdisch a.k.a. Peter Draws

PeterDraws
www.peterdraws.com

Copyright 2014 by Peter Deligdisch

Title "Between the Lines" by Eva Kernan Freire

ISBN: 978-1-495-33711-6

Dedicated to my loving friends and family who
continue to support me and my dreams despite my best efforts to
both expect the worst, and make the worst of it when it happens.

Instructions: Color between the lines.

Or don't. Whatever.
This is your book now.
Just have a good time with it.

If you are using markers, you may wish to place scrap paper between the pages to prevent bleed-through to the next page.

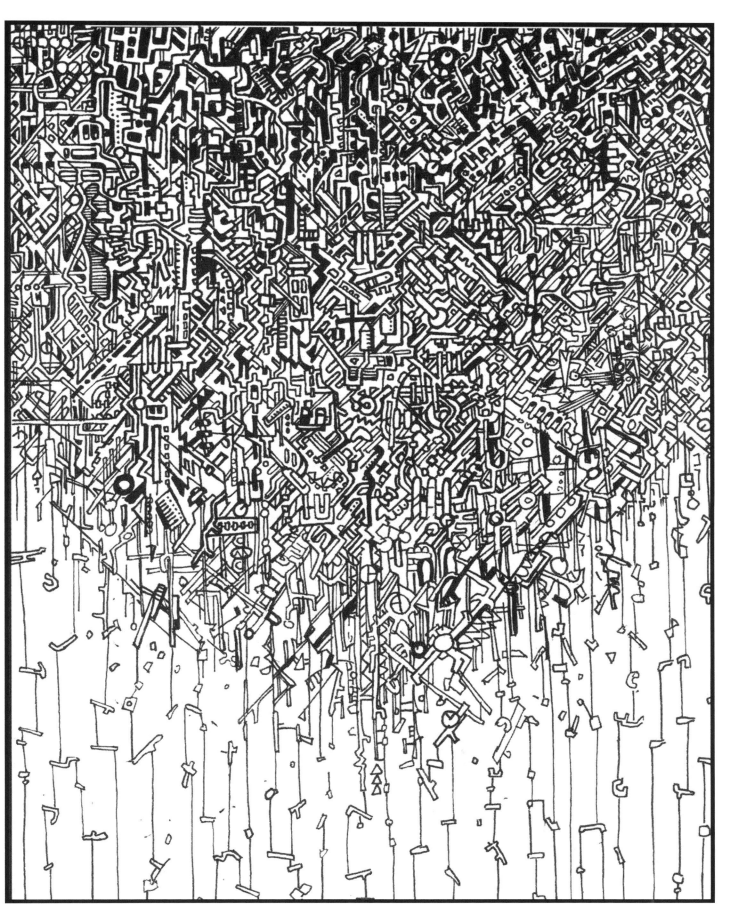